The · Life Cycle · Series

The Life Cycle of a

SALMON

© Natalie Fobes

Bobbie Kalman & Rebecca Sjonger

Crabtree Publishing Company

www.crabtreebooks.com

The Life Cycle Series

A Bobbie Kalman Book

Dedicated by Rebecca Sjonger
To the fish-loving Black family!

Editor-in-Chief
Bobbie Kalman

Writing team
Bobbie Kalman
Rebecca Sjonger

Substantive editor
Kathryn Smithyman

Project editor
Michael Hodge

Editors
Molly Aloian
Robin Johnson
Kelley MacAulay

Design
Margaret Amy Salter

Production coordinator
Heather Fitzpatrick

Photo research
Crystal Foxton

Consultant
Patricia Loesche, Ph.D., Animal Behavior Program,
Department of Psychology, University of Washington

Illustrations
All illustrations by Margaret Amy Salter except:
Barbara Bedell: pages 18 (top), 22 (shrimp), 23 (orca)
Diane Rome Peebles: page 22 (herring)
Tiffany Wybouw: page 23 (bottlenose dolphin)

Photographs
Steven Kazlowki/Peter Arnold/Alpha Presse: page 28 (top)
Kevin Schafer/Peter Arnold/Alpha Presse: page 24
© Bernard, George/Animals Animals - Earth Scenes: page 10
Bruce Coleman Inc.: Brandon Cole: page 30
© Natalie Fobes: title page, pages 3, 5, 6, 18, 20, 22 (bottom), 23, 25 (top), 26 (top), 27, 28 (bottom)
iStockphoto.com: Christine Davis: page 11
Photo Researchers, Inc.: Herve Berthoule/Jacana: page 12 (bottom); David R. Frazier: page 29
SeaPics.com: © Patrick Clayton: page 15; © Mark Conlin: front cover; © Daniel W. Gotshall:
    pages 4, 7 (bottom); © Chris Huss: pages 12 (top), 19 (top), 21 (top), 26 (bottom);
    © Steven Kazlowski: page 31 (top); © Jeff Mondragon: pages 16, 19 (bottom)
Visuals Unlimited: Ken Lucas: page 22 (top); Dr. Marli Miller: pages 7 (top), 21 (bottom);
    Glenn M. Oliver: page 14 (left)
Other images by Adobe Image Library, Digital Vision, and Photodisc

Library and Archives Canada Cataloguing in Publication

Kalman, Bobbie, date.
    The life cycle of a salmon / Bobbie Kalman & Rebecca Sjonger.
(The life cycle series)
Includes index.
ISBN-13: 978-0-7787-0631-1 (bound)
ISBN-10: 0-7787-0631-1 (bound)
ISBN-13: 978-0-7787-0705-9 (pbk.)
ISBN-10: 0-7787-0705-9 (pbk.)
    1. Salmon--Life cycles--Juvenile literature. I. Sjonger, Rebecca
II. Title. III. Series: Life cycle
QL638.S2K34 2006   j597.5'6   C2006-904095-8

Library of Congress Cataloging-in-Publication Data

Kalman, Bobbie.
    The life cycle of a salmon / Bobbie Kalman & Rebecca Sjonger.
    p. cm. -- (The life cycle series)
    Includes index.
    ISBN-13: 978-0-7787-0631-1 (rlb)
    ISBN-10: 0-7787-0631-1 (rlb)
    ISBN-13: 978-0-7787-0705-9 (pb)
    ISBN-10: 0-7787-0705-9 (pb)
    1. Salmon--Juvenile literature.   I. Sjonger, Rebecca. II. Title.
QL638.S2K34 2007
597.5'6--dc22
                                        2006018068
                                        LC

Crabtree Publishing Company

www.crabtreebooks.com   1-800-387-7650

Published in Canada
Crabtree Publishing
616 Welland Ave.
St. Catharines, ON
L2M 5V6

Published in the United States
Crabtree Publishing
PMB16A
350 Fifth Ave., Suite 3308
New York, NY 10118

Published in the United Kingdom
Crabtree Publishing
White Cross Mills
High Town, Lancaster
LA1 4XS

Published in Australia
Crabtree Publishing
386 Mt. Alexander Rd.
Ascot Vale (Melbourne)
VIC 3032

Contents

© Natalie Fobes

What are salmon?

Salmon are **fish**. Fish are **vertebrates**. A vertebrate is an animal that has a **backbone**. A backbone is a row of bones in the middle of an animal's back. Like most fish, salmon are **bony fish**. Bony fish have hard skeletons.

These salmon are bony fish. Clown fish, eels, goldfish, and most other fish are also bony fish.

Keeping their cool

Fish are **cold-blooded animals**. The body temperatures of cold-blooded animals change as the temperatures of their surroundings change. A salmon that is in cool water has a lower body temperature than a salmon that is in warm water.

This pink salmon is swimming in a cool river.

© Natalie Fobes

Salmon relations

Salmon belong to a family of fish called *Salmonidae*. Other members of this family include grayling, whitefish, char, and trout. Salmon and trout are closely related. Scientists do not always agree on whether trout are actually a species of salmon!

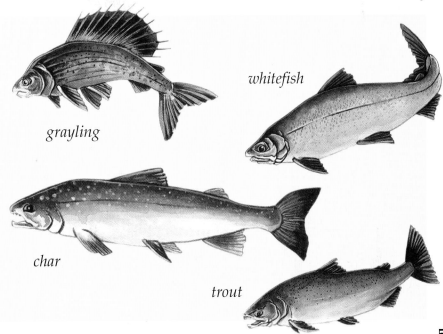

grayling

whitefish

char

trout

Fresh water and salt water

Young salmon live in freshwater habitats.

The natural place where an animal lives is called its **habitat**. Some fish live in **freshwater** habitats, such as rivers and lakes. Other fish live in **saltwater** habitats, such as oceans. Fresh water contains little salt, whereas salt water contains a lot of salt. Most freshwater fish cannot survive in salt water and most saltwater fish cannot live in fresh water.

Fantastic fish

Salmon are found in North America, Europe, and Asia. Salmon are different from most other fish because they spend part of their lives in fresh water and part of their lives in salt water. Young salmon live in freshwater rivers and lakes, whereas most fully grown salmon live in oceans.

This fully grown salmon lives in a saltwater habitat.

An important stop

Salmon cannot swim directly from fresh water to salt water. They must first swim through **estuaries**. An estuary forms where a river meets an ocean. In an estuary, there is a mixture of fresh water and salt water. The mixture of water helps a salmon's body adjust to salt water before it enters an ocean. Salmon also stay in estuaries to adjust to fresh water before they return to their freshwater habitats.

Before entering oceans, salmon swim through estuaries, such as the Umpqua River estuary in Oregon.

Fresh water forever

Some salmon are **landlocked**. Landlocked salmon live in lakes and rivers that do not connect to oceans. These fish spend their entire lives in freshwater habitats. The bodies of water in which they live are often deep and cold.

Landlocked salmon, such as this kokanee salmon, are also known as lake-form salmon.

Salmon species

There are eight main **species**, or types, of salmon—Atlantic, chinook, chum, pink, sockeye, coho, steelhead, and masu. Atlantic salmon live part of their lives in fresh water and part of their lives in the Atlantic Ocean. The other seven species make up a group called Pacific salmon. These salmon live part of their lives in fresh water and part of their lives in the Pacific Ocean.

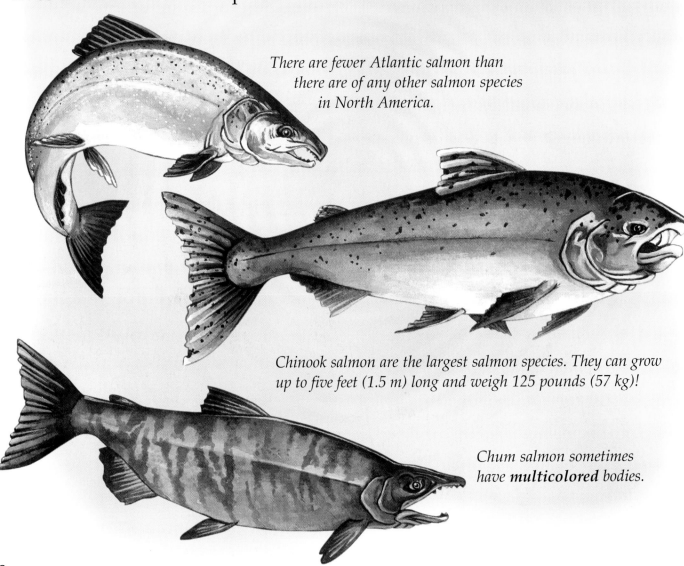

There are fewer Atlantic salmon than there are of any other salmon species in North America.

Chinook salmon are the largest salmon species. They can grow up to five feet (1.5 m) long and weigh 125 pounds (57 kg)!

*Chum salmon sometimes have **multicolored** bodies.*

Pink salmon are the smallest salmon species. They are about 21 inches (53 cm) long and often weigh less than five pounds (2 kg).

Sockeye salmon are also known as red salmon because their bodies turn bright red.

Coho salmon are commonly known as silverside salmon because the sides of their bodies are silver.

Steelhead salmon are also called coastal rainbow trout. They are more closely related to salmon than to trout, however.

Masu salmon are also called Japanese salmon because they live mainly in waters around Japan.

A salmon's body

A salmon has a sleekly shaped body. This shape allows a salmon to move easily through water. The salmon swims using body parts called **fins**. It has strong muscles in its body. The muscles control the fins. They also give the salmon a lot of power. Salmon are strong swimmers!

*A salmon has a pair of **pectoral fins**.*

*Gill covers are flaps of skin that protect a salmon's **gills**.*

*A salmon smells with **nares**. Nares are like nostrils.*

Different salmon species have gums of different colors.

Great gills

Like all fish, salmon have body parts called gills. Gills allow fish to breathe under water. Water enters a salmon's body through its mouth and exits through its gills. As water flows through the gills, the gills take in **oxygen**. Oxygen is a gas found in air and water that all animals must breathe to survive.

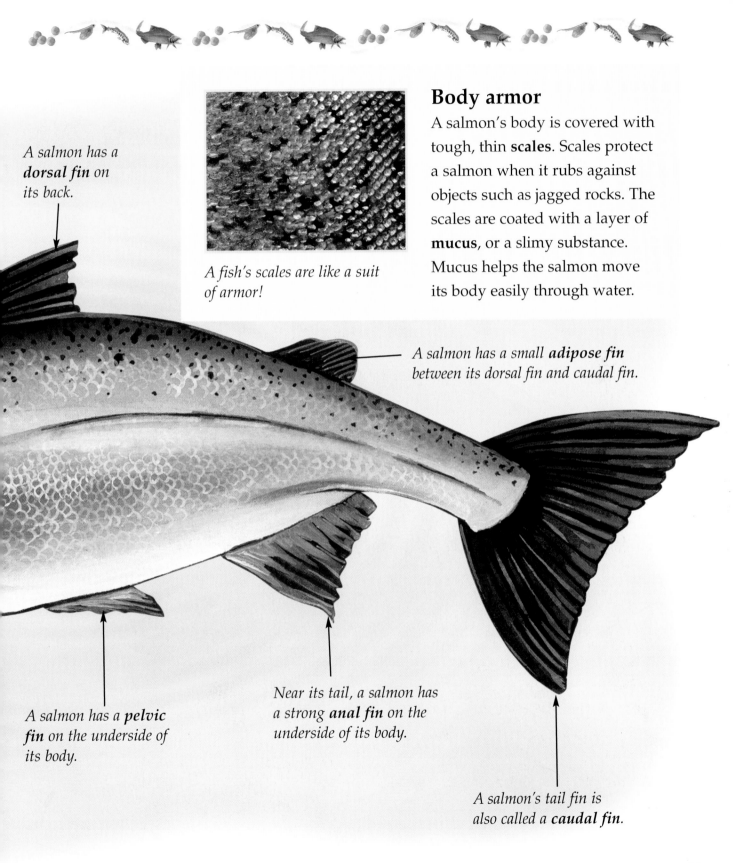

A salmon has a **dorsal fin** on its back.

A fish's scales are like a suit of armor!

Body armor

A salmon's body is covered with tough, thin **scales**. Scales protect a salmon when it rubs against objects such as jagged rocks. The scales are coated with a layer of **mucus**, or a slimy substance. Mucus helps the salmon move its body easily through water.

A salmon has a small **adipose fin** between its dorsal fin and caudal fin.

A salmon has a **pelvic fin** on the underside of its body.

Near its tail, a salmon has a strong **anal fin** on the underside of its body.

A salmon's tail fin is also called a **caudal fin**.

11

What is a life cycle?

All salmon species have similar life cycles.

A **life cycle** is a series of changes that every animal goes through. Early in its life cycle, an animal is born or hatches from an egg. The animal grows and changes until it becomes **mature**. A mature animal can **reproduce**, or make babies with another animal of the same species.

Life spans

A life cycle is not the same as a **life span**. A life span is the length of time an animal is alive. Different species of salmon have different life spans. For example, coho salmon live for two to four years, whereas chinook salmon live for three to six years. Atlantic salmon usually have longer life spans than Pacific salmon do. Most Atlantic salmon live for about six years.

The oldest recorded Atlantic salmon lived for thirteen years!

The life cycle of salmon

Salmon begin their life cycles inside eggs as **embryos**, or developing animals. Tiny salmon called **alevins** hatch from the eggs. Alevins cannot swim. After about a month, alevins grow into **fry** that can swim and find food. Some species of fry develop **parr marks**, or spots. These fry are known as **parr**. When fry and parr are ready to leave their freshwater homes, they are called **smolts**. Smolts swim to saltwater habitats where they continue to grow. Fully grown salmon return to fresh water, where they become mature.

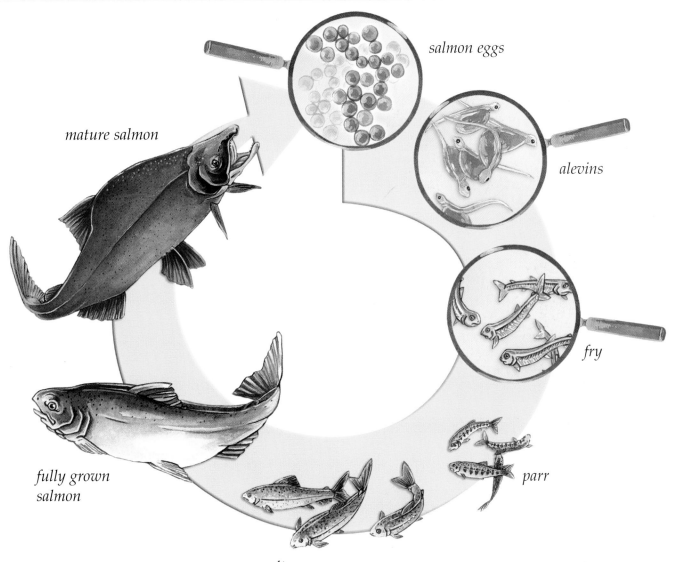

salmon eggs

alevins

fry

mature salmon

parr

fully grown salmon

smolts

Eggs and embryos

A female salmon lays eggs in a **redd**, or nest. She uses her tail to dig a redd in the gravel at the bottom of a stream or a river. The eggs blend in with the gravel and stay hidden from hungry animals. Fresh water washes over the eggs, keeping them cool and clean.

Salmon eggs must stay clean and cool to keep the embryos inside them healthy.

Helpful trees

Trees help keep salmon eggs healthy. The roots of trees that grow along rivers and streams stop soil from sliding into the water. As a result, the water flowing around salmon eggs stays clean. Trees also provide shade, which keeps the eggs from becoming too warm.

Growing on the inside

Salmon eggs are small and soft. The eggs are reddish-orange in color. Each egg contains an embryo. There is a **yolk sac** attached to each embryo. The yolk sac holds **yolk**, which is the embryo's food. As the embryo grows,

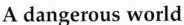

it develops two large, black eyes that can be seen through the egg. Most embryos grow inside their eggs for one or two months. Some embryos take longer to grow, however. Embryos in very cold water may stay inside their eggs for up to five months.

A dangerous world

Salmon eggs face many dangers, even in the safety of a redd. If an animal disturbs the redd, the delicate embryos inside it may die. Fish such as trout search for salmon redds and eat the eggs. Salmon sometimes make redds in shallow water that dries up when warm weather arrives. Embryos cannot survive in eggs that are not under water.

Birds such as ducks and fish such as this trout eat salmon eggs when they find them.

Alevins

Many alevins hatch from their eggs in early spring. Alevins do not look like adult salmon. Their bodies are only about one inch (2.5 cm) long. They do not have fins, and they cannot swim. They use their tiny tails to push themselves short distances through water.

Laying low

Many **predators** eat alevins. Predators are animals that hunt and eat other animals. Fish and birds are alevin predators. Alevins keep safe by staying in their redds. It is difficult for predators to see alevins among the gravel in their redds.

Sac lunch

An alevin does not need to look for food to eat. It gets all the **nutrients** it needs from its yolk sac. The yolk sac is attached to the underside of the alevin's body. The alevin grows quickly as it gets nutrients from its yolk sac.

So long, redd!

After four to six weeks, an alevin has used up all the yolk inside its yolk sac. By the time the alevin runs out of yolk, its fins have grown enough to allow it to swim out of its redd and find food. When a young salmon leaves the redd in which it hatched, it begins the next stage of its life cycle.

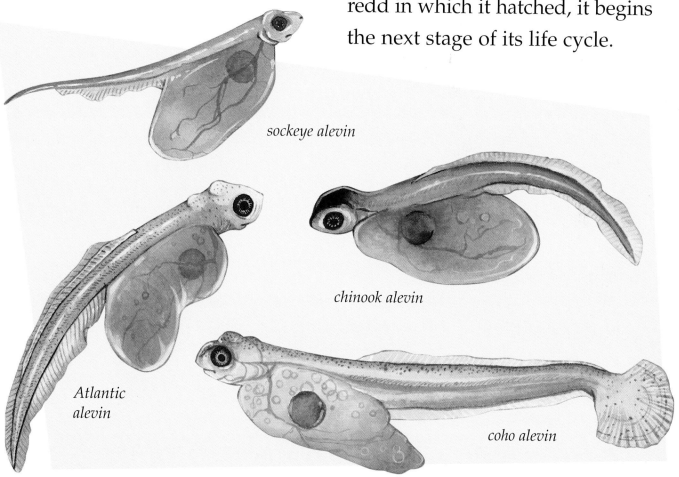

sockeye alevin

chinook alevin

Atlantic alevin

coho alevin

Every alevin has a yolk sac. The yolk sac becomes smaller as the alevin grows. When the yolk sac is empty, it becomes part of the alevin's body.

Fry and parr

© Natalie Fobes

When young salmon swim out of their redds to find food, they are called fry. Fry have fins, teeth, and scales. They are twice as big as alevins are. Fry must eat a lot so that they can continue to grow. At first, most fry eat **plankton**, which are tiny plants and animals floating in water. As fry continue to grow, they start to eat larger foods such as insects and fish eggs.

These coho fry eat plankton as they swim.

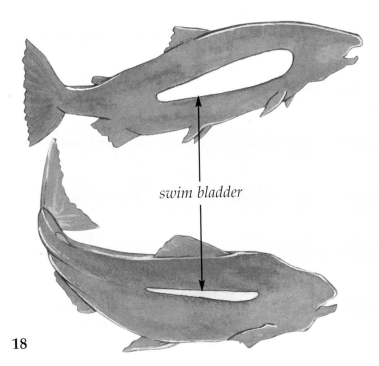

swim bladder

Swim bladders

When fry begin to swim, they use their **swim bladders** for the first time. A swim bladder is a balloonlike part inside a fish's body that allows the fish to float. Fish use their swim bladders to move up and down in water. To move toward the water's surface, a fish takes air into the swim bladder through its mouth. When the fish lets air out of the swim bladder through its gills, it moves downward through water.

Safety schools

Birds and large fish often eat fry. One way fry stay safe from predators is by swimming together. Hundreds of fry of the same species may form a **school**, or group of fish. Swimming in a school helps keep fry safe. Predators may confuse the group of small fish for one large fish and leave the fry alone!

Protective parr marks

When most fry are a few months old, they become parr. Parr have dark, oval parr marks on their bodies. Parr marks are **camouflage** that help hide parr among rocks and weeds in their freshwater habitats. Animals with camouflage have colors, patterns, or **textures** on their bodies that help them blend in with their surroundings. Some fry species, such as pink salmon, do not develop parr marks. They are never called parr.

These chinook fry are safer in a school than they would be on their own.

Dark spots make parr less noticeable to predators.

Smolts

© Natalie Fobes

When fry and parr are ready to leave their freshwater habitats, they are called smolts. Most smolts are between one and six inches (2.5-15 cm) long and weigh less than four ounces (113 g). Smolts look like small adult salmon. If they had parr marks, the marks have faded. Their bodies are now a pale, silver color. This color provides camouflage in ocean waters.

On the move

Smolts **migrate** from fresh water to salt water. An animal that migrates travels from one place to another for a specific purpose. A smolt migrates to the ocean to find food. Some species, including chum salmon smolts, migrate during their first few months of life. Other species, including Atlantic salmon smolts, live in fresh water for up to three years before they migrate.

Following the current

A smolt migrates toward salt water by following the water's **current**. A current is the natural movement of water in a certain direction. Currents in rivers flow toward oceans. The smolt follows the water's current until it enters an estuary.

These smolts are entering an estuary.

Estuary life

Smolts live in estuaries for weeks. Before entering the ocean, smolts must become used to salt water. There is plenty of food in most estuaries, so smolts quickly grow larger and stronger. Estuaries sometimes **flood**, or overflow. If an estuary floods before the smolts are ready to live in salt water, they can be swept into salt water too soon and die.

Many smolts enter the Pacific Ocean through this estuary in California.

Into the ocean

When a smolt enters the ocean, it is a salmon. While living in salt water, salmon may swim over one thousand miles (1609 km) out into the ocean in search of **prey**. Prey are animals that predators hunt and eat. Salmon find a wide variety of prey in oceans. Using their senses of smell and sight, salmon find fish such as herring, **crustaceans** such as shrimp, and larger animals such as squid. Salmon grow rapidly after entering saltwater habitats. They are soon fully grown.

*Most salmon swim far away from **coasts**. Coho salmon are found mainly near coasts, however.*

shrimp

herring

Fully grown salmon eat large prey such as opalescent squid.

How long in the ocean?
Different salmon species spend different lengths of time in the ocean. Masu salmon often spend just one winter in the ocean. These chinook salmon may live in the ocean for up to seven years, however.

© Natalie Fobes

Out of sight

To avoid predators, fully grown salmon have a type of camouflage called **countershading**. Animals with countershading have dark backs and light bellies. Having countershading makes salmon hard to see in deep ocean waters. A predator swimming below a salmon may look up and not notice the salmon. The salmon's pale belly and sides help it blend in with the sunny surface of the water. A predator swimming above the salmon may not see it because the salmon's dark back blends in with the dark ocean floor below.

Many ocean-dwelling fish, such as this pink salmon, have countershading.

New predators

In addition to having many prey in oceans, salmon also have many predators. Ocean animals that eat salmon include dolphins, sea lions, seals, sharks, and whales. Seabirds swoop down from the sky and catch salmon that swim near the water's surface.

bottlenose dolphin

salmon shark

orca

On the run

After spending between one and seven years growing in the ocean, fully grown salmon are nearly mature. Before salmon can mate, they must journey back to the areas where they hatched. This long, hard journey is called a **salmon run**. Many salmon begin their salmon run in autumn. It may take months to complete the run.

Back to the estuary

Fully grown salmon travel back to the same estuaries they used when they entered salt water as smolts. Scientists believe that salmon can tell which estuary to enter by its smell! In the same way that smolts waited in estuaries to adjust to salt water, fully grown salmon stay in estuaries until their bodies adjust to fresh water.

These fully grown salmon are returning to the freshwater habitats in which they hatched.

The return trip

During a salmon run, salmon must travel **upstream**, or against the current. Swimming against a current makes it difficult for salmon to move forward. While they are migrating upstream, salmon stop eating and use all their energy to complete their difficult journey. By the time the salmon finish the salmon run, they are mature.

*In species such as sockeye salmon, the **snouts** of the males become sharply hooked during a salmon run.*

Super swimmers!

While swimming upstream, salmon use their strong tails and other fins to push their bodies against the current. They thrust themselves over obstacles such as logs and rocks. Salmon can even leap up waterfalls! Predators such as bears, birds, and otters hunt along the rivers and streams where the salmon are traveling. As the salmon leap into the air, these animals catch them.

This grizzly bear has caught a leaping salmon.

Ready to spawn

Before salmon reproduce, their bodies change color for the final time in their life cycles. To attract partners, salmon turn a variety of bright colors as they travel. Their brightly colored bodies may also frighten away other fish. By the time salmon reach their **spawning grounds**, or the places where they began their lives, they look very different than they looked in the ocean.

The bodies of mature sockeye salmon change color, but their heads do not.

Readying the redd

Salmon reproduce by spawning. To spawn, a female salmon uses her tail to dig a shallow redd. She then lays her eggs in the redd. The movements the female makes while she digs her redd attract male salmon. A male swims into the redd and **fertilizes** the eggs. With a swish of her tail, the female covers the fertilized eggs with gravel. If the female has more eggs to lay, she may dig more redds. The same male will fertilize those eggs, as well.

Female salmon lay between 1500 and 10,000 eggs each time they spawn.

The end of the cycle

Once the salmon run and spawning are complete, the salmon are hungry and tired. Salmon may stay near their eggs to protect them, but the salmon die long before the alevins hatch. The bodies of the dead salmon gradually **decay**, or break down, in the water around their eggs.

Decaying salmon add nutrients to the water, which makes the water healthy for eggs, alevins, and fry.

Exceptions to the rule

Some steelhead and Atlantic salmon do not die after spawning. These fish rest and then swim back to their saltwater habitats. They may grow very large in the oceans. Some of these salmon are able to return to their spawning grounds a second or even a third time.

*The bodies of **kelts**, or Atlantic salmon that have spawned and then returned to salt water, are darker than the bodies of other Atlantic salmon are.*

27

Dangers to salmon

This fisher's net is full of coho salmon.

People's actions threaten salmon **populations**. A population is the total number of one species living in an area. Some people **overfish** salmon. Overfishing occurs when people take too many of one species of fish from an area. In these areas, the number of salmon caught each year is greater than the number of alevins that hatch each year. As a result, salmon populations are getting smaller.

Fish farms

People **cultivate** salmon on **fish farms**. To cultivate salmon means to raise them and sell them as food. Fish farms are made up of underwater cages that hold huge numbers of salmon. Species of large, cultivated salmon sometimes escape their cages and eat all the prey in the habitats of smaller, wild salmon. Escaped salmon may also introduce diseases to wild salmon. The wild salmon can become sick and may even die.

© Natalie Fobes

Dirty waters

People also destroy salmon habitats. Some salmon habitats are destroyed when people **clear** land. To clear land means to remove the trees and other plants from it. When land is cleared, a lot of soil slides into waterways and makes the water muddy. Alevins and fry cannot survive in muddy water. People also **pollute** the water in which salmon live. To pollute water means to make it dirty. Polluted water makes salmon sick. Salmon may even die because of polluted water in their habitats.

Blocked routes

People build **dams** along rivers to control the flow of water. Salmon that use the rivers as migration routes cannot reach their spawning grounds. These salmon do not lay eggs before they die. Salmon populations get smaller because fewer eggs are laid each year.

*A salmon may be injured or killed if it swims through a dam's **turbines**, or machinery.*

Helping salmon

Conservation groups are working hard to protect salmon and their habitats. The people who belong to conservation groups are trying to make governments and other people aware of the threats that salmon face. These groups have convinced the governments in the United States and Canada to pass laws and to create programs to help protect salmon and their habitats.

Climbing ladders

Some dam builders have designed **fish ladders**, such as the one shown right. Fish ladders provide salmon with routes around the dams. Strong salmon are able to use fish ladders. Weaker salmon are not, however. Some people catch weaker salmon and carry them around the dams. Other people are working to stop the building of dams along salmon migration routes.

Hatching a plan

Fish hatcheries are human-made places where fish eggs develop and hatch. Fish hatcheries help increase the number of salmon in the wild. They release young salmon into the wild to help increase salmon populations.

Only a small number of salmon can be released into a habitat, however, and there can be no other salmon already in that habitat. If there are too many salmon in one habitat, there will not be enough food for all of them.

These men are working at a salmon hatchery.

How can you help?

Brainstorm ways that you can help salmon. If you live near a salmon habitat, consider starting a cleanup project in the rivers and streams in your area. If you live far from natural salmon habitats, you can still help by cleaning up nearby ponds and streams. Water flows from one waterway to another. Your efforts may help salmon that live far away!

Glossary

Note: Boldfaced words that are defined in the text may not appear in the glossary.

coast An area of land next to a body of water

conservation group A group of people who work to protect animals and their habitats

crustacean An animal that has a hard shell and at least four pairs of legs and two pairs of antennae

dam A structure that blocks the flow of water

fertilize To add sperm to an egg

multicolored Describing something that has many colors

nutrients The natural substances that an animal needs to grow and stay healthy

redd A shallow nest dug into gravel by a female salmon

snout A nose and jaw that sticks out of an animal's face

texture The look and feel of the surface of something—how rough or smooth it is

Index

1 2 3 4 5 6 7 8 9 0   Printed in the U.S.A. 5 4 3 2 1 0 9 8 7 6